BIRD WATCHING

by
Gareth Thomas

FRANKLIN WATTS
London

Contents

Introduction

Birdwatching is an exciting hobby, which you will probably start by watching the birds near your home. Later, when you have seen most of your local birds, you may want to look further afield, and watch unfamiliar birds in woods, mountains and at wet places.

You will soon find out there is much more to birdwatching than just identifying birds, and this book will help you to discover new ways of learning more about them.

Things you can do

If you collect feathers, feet, wings, skulls and pellets they will help you understand how different birds have *adapted* to their way of life. You can find out a lot about bird behaviour by watching patiently, and you can set up simple experiments in your garden to find out more about birds' senses and habits, and then compare them to other animals (including yourself).

Make some feeding equipment, a pool and dustbox, and you can watch and record how different *species* feed, drink and bathe.

Above all, birds are able to fly, and so have adapted themselves to life all over the world. Many *migratory* birds are able to spend time each year in different parts of the world, often thousands of kilometres apart.

Away from home, you can look at the *habitats* birds live in. Different species are specially adapted to woodlands, water areas, grasslands or other places. You can do field work to count or estimate the numbers of feeding or roosting flocks in an area. You can also take a *census* of breeding birds with conspicuous nests, like rooks, or *territory*-holding birds like blackbirds which sing from obvious *song posts*.

Lastly, if you want to develop your interest in birds further, join a club. There may be a local club in your area, or you can join *The Young Ornithologists' Club*. This club is for people up to the age of 15 and has a quarterly magazine. It runs projects, courses and competitions, and holds nationwide meetings.

Write to: The Young Ornithologists' Club, The Lodge, Sandy, Bedfordshire SG19 2DL.

1 : Starting Birdwatching

If you are just starting bird-watching there are a few basic rules that are helpful to know. Firstly, make sure you wear the right clothes. There is nothing worse than feeling cold and wet when you have to keep still.

If it is chilly wrap up well with sweaters and a warm, waterproof jacket, or carry a folded plastic mac. If you have to walk over rough ground, wear stout shoes or boots, and wellingtons are essential in marshy areas. Try not to wear brightly coloured clothes. Soft colours, especially greens and browns, will give you more *camouflage*.

KEEP TO THE COUNTRY CODE (see page 9). If you want to watch birds away from public places, find out who owns the land and ask their permission first. Choose a good position that will give you some cover. Look across fields from gaps in hedges or gateways, so you are not too conspicuous.

In woodland sit quietly under a tree, particularly if it is near a clearing, or water. A surprising number of birds will show themselves. At gravel

pits, reservoirs, lakes, or along the coast, try to hide behind banks and sea walls.

When walking in open spaces like heaths and moors, keep an eye on the horizon. You may glimpse large birds there, or spot distant flocks. Cars make great *hides* in open country, so it is well worth using a car in this way whenever it is possible.

You will hear lots of bird

▲ Make use of natural cover when birdwatching. The birds shown in this picture are: black-headed gulls, blue tit, carrion crow, kestrel, magpie, male pheasant, robin, song thrush and wood pigeons. Can you identify them?

noises in woods and at watery sites. You should identify the 'pink-pink' call of the chaffinch fairly easily, and blackbirds are often easy to spot on their song posts. However, you will need some patience before you find out that the loud song coming from the undergrowth, for example, may belong to a tiny wren.

Useful equipment

A *notebook* and *pencil* are essential. The notebook should be small enough to fit into your pocket. Many people later rewrite their records (field notes) into a permanent record book at home.

When you see a bird you cannot identify, do a quick *field sketch* (see opposite). Draw in any striking *plumage* details or characteristics such as wing bars, eye stripes, long tails or pointed wings. Check these *field characters* later in a field guide. You will also need your notebook to record activities and bird 'counts'.

REMEMBER TO WRITE YOUR OBSERVATIONS DOWN AT ONCE, or you will probably forget them after a few minutes.

If you take birdwatching at all seriously, you will need a pair of *binoculars*. There are some good, inexpensive ones available, but it's best to go to the shop with someone who knows something about them. Most shopkeepers will let you try them out in the shop doorway by looking at objects in the street.

Avoid binoculars where the images are distorted at the edges with coloured 'haloes'. Binoculars are specified by their *magnification* and the *diameter of the lens*. Good general-purpose binoculars are 8×30, 8×35 and 8×40. Remember that you wear them around your neck, so don't get anything too heavy.

To record bird calls or songs,

Equipment

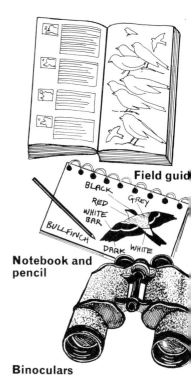

Field guide

Notebook and pencil

Binoculars

you can use an ordinary portable *cassette recorder*. If you want to take photographs for your permanent record book, an inexpensive 'instamatic' camera will give quite good results.

A good *field guide* is well worth buying, although, at a pinch, you can look at one in your local library. The best field guides have drawings and descriptions of all the birds

Making a field sketch

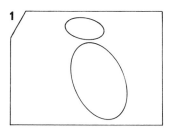

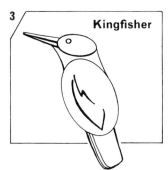

Kingfisher

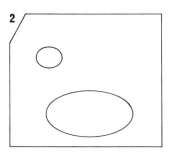

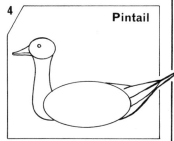

Pintail

▲ Draw two ovals for the head and body showing relative positions (1 & 2).

▲ Join the ovals and fill in details such as plumage, colour, beak and tail (3 & 4).

you are likely to see.

ABOVE ALL, PLEASE RE-MEMBER THAT ALL WILD BIRDS, THEIR NESTS AND EGGS ARE PROTECTED BY LAW. You must not collect eggs nor remove nests in the breeding season. Be very careful not to disturb nesting or feeding birds, especially during cold winter weather when food is scarce and feeding time is very valuable.

The country code

● **Keep to public footpaths and roads.**
● **Ask permission before entering private land.**
● **Close gates after you.**
● **Don't leave litter or start fires.**
● **Don't destroy vegetation or disturb animals.**

2 : What is a Bird?

About 150 million years ago the first birds took to the air. Unlike the reptiles from which they *evolved*, birds are warm-blooded, have feathers, and most can fly. The young hatch from hard-shelled eggs and are usually looked after by their parents for a time after hatching.

Parts of a bird (bullfinch)

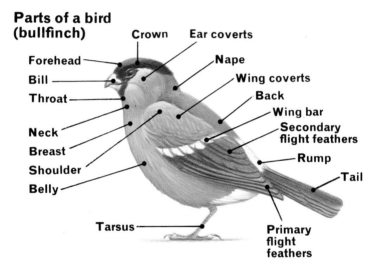

METABOLIC RATES	BIRDS	HUMANS
Temperature	40–42°C	? °C
Pulse rate	300 per minute for a chicken	? per minute
Breathing rate (when resting)	30 per minute for a pigeon	? per minute
Breathing rate (after flying or running)	450 per minute for a pigeon	? per minute after a 100 m run

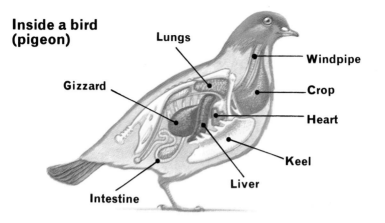

Inside a bird (pigeon)

- Lungs
- Windpipe
- Gizzard
- Crop
- Heart
- Keel
- Liver
- Intestine

The body processes of birds work very quickly, mainly because they need a lot of energy for flying. The chart below left shows some facts about the *metabolic rates* of birds. Measure your own rates and compare them.

If you find a dead bird, try looking for the following features. BUT ALWAYS BE CAREFUL WHEN HANDLING DEAD ANIMALS. WEAR GLOVES AND MAKE SURE YOU WASH YOUR HANDS THOROUGHLY AFTER TOUCHING THEM.

The head has a flexible neck, a pair of nostrils and two large eyes, each with three eyelids. You should find the two ears below and behind the eyes under some feathers called *ear coverts*. The *bill* (beak) and claws have horny coverings of *keratin* – like your finger nails.

The largest wing feathers are called the *primary* and *secondary flight feathers* (see page 12). Beneath the soft *contour feathers* the body is covered by a thin skin. Above the base of the tail is the *oil* or *preen gland*. The legs and feet have scales.

The drawing above shows some of a bird's internal organs. The bony *keel* supports two large breast muscles, one on either side.

The heart is relatively large, but the lungs are quite small. Birds breathe not only by passing air into their lungs, but also into *air sacs*, some of which extend into the bones.

Birds do not have any teeth for chewing their food. Instead, they have a hard muscular *gizzard*, often containing pieces of grit for crushing food.

11

Next time you get the chance to look at a 'chicken wing', see how well developed the 'arm' bones are. One 'finger' is very small, and two are missing. The second and third 'fingers' are enlarged and joined together. Humans have five free-moving fingers for grasping objects, but birds use their bills and feet for this.

Crack open one of the 'arm' bones and see the large hollow spaces inside. Because of them, a bird bone weighs less than a similar-sized reptile or mammal bone. Why do you think this is useful to the bird?

Preserving dead birds
If dead birds are fresh and unmangled, you can preserve them. REMEMBER ALWAYS TO WEAR RUBBER GLOVES.

The following method is best for birds smaller than a carrion crow. Your specimens should last for several years.

You will need some normal *formaldehyde* (formalin) solution, and a *hypodermic syringe and needle*. FORMALIN IS A POISON AND YOU MUST ONLY USE IT UNDER SUPERVISION. IF YOU GET SOME IN YOUR EYES WASH THEM IMMEDIATELY WITH WATER.

For finch-sized birds mix one part of formaldehyde solution to two parts of water. Larger birds will need one part of solution to one part of water. Inject the solution via the *eye socket*, into the *chest*, *breast muscles* and *belly* until the preservative begins to ooze out of the body.

Leave the body to air in a dry, breezy place for a few days, WELL OUT OF THE WAY OF ANY OTHER ANIMAL OR YOUNG CHILD. Then you can put it in a box or case.

Flight feather for flying and steering

Filoplume

Contour feather for warmth and streamlining

Down feather – some birds like ducks have these for extra warmth

Collecting skulls

You may be lucky and find some bird skulls that are clean and white. If not, boil the head of a dead bird in water and simmer it until you can scrape away the flesh and feathers. Whiten the skull in diluted household bleach overnight.

Try not to lose the small bones from the angle of the upper and lower jaws, and glue these in place when dry. Keep your skulls in a display box and label them.

Feathers

The picture shows the main feathers and what they are for. *Filoplumes* are the tiny, hair-like feathers you can see in the skin after plucking.

Colourful feathers are used for signalling (*displaying*) to

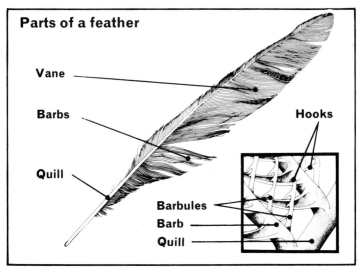

Parts of a feather

Vane

Barbs

Quill

Hooks

Barbules

Barb

Quill

other birds. Dull ones are for camouflage. Feathers also keep the body dry. Pour water over a large feather and see what happens.

A feather is made up of a central *quill* with *vanes* on either side. If you can, look at a section of vanes under a hand lens or a low power microscope. Each vane has lots of *barbs*, with many *barbules* attached. Each barbule has lots of *hooks* which lock onto the hooks of neighbouring barbules.

Feet

Different types of bird have differently shaped feet, depending on the way they live. There are five main types, each with its own characteristics:

Perching (blackbird). Three slender toes pointing forward and one back.

Climbing (green woodpecker). Two slender toes pointing forward and two back.

Walking and scratching (pheasant). Muscular toes with short claws.

Holding (kestrel). Muscular, with long *talons* for holding prey.

Swimming, either *webbed* (mallard), or *lobed* (coot).

Collecting feet

Cut the foot off a dead bird at the first leg joint up from the toes. To display it, you could

▲ Waterbirds have webbed feet. The webs of skin between the toes make an efficient paddle.

▲ Birds of prey have muscular legs and sharp talons for gripping their prey.

▲ Perching birds have slender toes, well-designed for walking, hopping and perching.

push some stiff wire through the foot and into a piece of thick balsa wood. Or you could pin or tape the foot onto a piece of card.

If the foot is hard and misshapen, leave it to soak in water until it is soft enough to mould back into its normal shape. Label with the species, place and date you found it, and add a short sentence about the foot, describing it and what it was used for.

How birds move on land

On land, birds can either *hop*, *walk*, *run* or *crawl*. Keep records of the ways you see different birds moving – some birds use more than one method.

A bird has to have its centre of gravity over its feet to balance properly. In a bird like a partridge, the legs are about half-way along the body, near the centre of gravity, so the body stands more or less parallel to the ground.

The legs of a cormorant, however, are set further back; to balance properly on land it has to stand very upright. The Manx shearwater has legs set so far back on its body that it cannot stand up at all. These birds usually have to move on land by crawling along on their bellies. How would you describe how you move and stand?

Making plaster casts of bird footprints

You will need:
A piece of cardboard 4 cm wide, and a *paper clip*.

How birds stand

Cormorant

Partridge

Manx shearwater

Making a plaster cast of a footprint

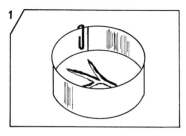

▲ Push a circle of cardboard into the mud around the print to a depth of 2 cm.

▲ Pour plaster of paris onto the footprint until it is level with the top of the card.

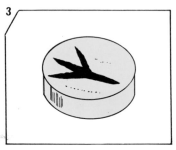

▲ When the plaster is set, you can paint the print black and the cast in another colour.

Plaster of paris from a chemist or art shop.

Look for good, clear footprints in firm muddy places, such as the edges of ponds. Or, you can create your own muddy area if you fill a tray with firm wet mud. Put the tray on the ground in your garden and sprinkle some food on it, so that birds will come and stand in the mud. This is a good way of making quite sure which species made the footprints.

When you have some good sharp prints, bend the cardboard into a circle and fasten the ends with the paper clip. Push it into the mud as shown in diagram 1 above.

Mix the plaster of paris with water into a thick creamy liquid. Pour it onto the footprint and leave it to set for about two hours. REMEMBER NOT TO POUR ANY SURPLUS PLASTER DOWN THE SINK, OR IT MAY SET THERE!

Remove the cast from the mud, take off the cardboard and sponge any mud off the cast. Write details of the species of bird, the date and place you found the footprint on the back of the cast in ink. These casts make good ornaments and paper weights.

3 : Bird Senses

Birds seem to have a poor sense of taste and smell, but their hearing, sight and touch are usually well developed.

Smell and taste

Of these two senses, most birds seem to have a better sense of taste than smell. One way of testing this is to mix up a strong solution of salt and water. Dip one piece of bread in the salt water and another piece in plain water. Put the pieces outside, about 30 cm apart. How many birds come to feed on each piece? How many stop feeding on the salty bread after appearing to 'taste' it?

Try this test again with pieces of bread soaked for a few seconds in a mixture of vinegar and water, and in ordinary water. How many birds seem to 'smell' the vinegary bread? Do they feed on it, or move away?

Touch and hearing

Birds are very sensitive to vibrations caused by movement. Nestlings will open their beaks if their parents land near the nest. Try tying one end of some string to a fence post, or the edge of a bird table. Pull

▲ Kiwis have very poor sight and use the nostrils on the end of their beak to smell out food. They may have the best sense of smell of all birds.

▼ The bristles around a night-jar's bill help it to locate the flying insects on which it feeds.

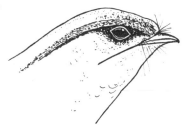

the string taut and anchor the other end to a firm object some distance away. When a bird lands on the bird table, pluck the string very gently. What happens?

17

Woodcock (all-round view)

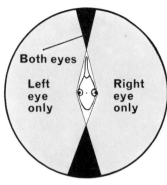

Owl (forward view only)

▲ Areas of binocular vision are shown in black, and monocular in grey. The white parts show the bird's 'blind' areas.

How well do birds hear? Tape record the song of a male songbird in its territory (see page 49), and then play the tape back to the bird. What happens? Does the bird think the tape recorder is a rival male? Does it sing back to it, or attack it?

Sight

This is the best developed sense in birds. Birds that are regularly hunted by *predators* have fairly narrow heads with eyes at the side. This gives them a good field of view out of each eye (*monocular vision*), but only a small field of view out of both eyes together (*binocular vision*).

Predatory birds like owls, however, have wide heads with both eyes directed forward. This gives them a good binocular field of view so they can accurately judge how far away their prey is.

Imagine you are in the middle of a circle. Look straight ahead and keep your head still. Shut your *left* eye. Hold your finger up and follow it as far *right* as you can with your *right* eye. Mark this point on a circle drawn on a piece of paper. With the left eye still shut, look as far *left* (over your nose) as you can with your *right* eye, and mark this point down. Now repeat the process with the *left* eye, keeping the *right* one shut. Join each of the four points at the centre of the circle. Shade in your binocular and monocular fields of view. Do you think people were once hunters, or were they hunted?

4: Food and Feeding

Birds eat all sorts of food. A bird that eats only plant food is called a *herbivore*. One that eats animals is called a *carnivore*. Birds that eat both are *omnivores*.

Here are some examples:
Herbivores:
Mute swan – waterweeds
Wood pigeon – clover
Carnivores:
Kestrel – vole
Kingfisher – fish
Omnivores:
Blackbird – worms and apples
Herring gull – grain and crabs

Food chains and webs

The link between sunlight (which helps plants to grow) and the final predator is called a *food chain*. The diagram below shows one type of food chain, and the following are also good examples:
First food chain:
Sunlight–grass–cow (herbivore)–man (carnivore).
Second food chain:
Sunlight–grass–wigeon (herbivore)–peregrine (carnivore).

Most animals, however, eat several kinds of food, and the links between them can be shown as a *food web*:

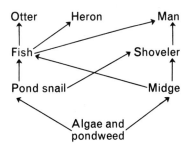

A food chain

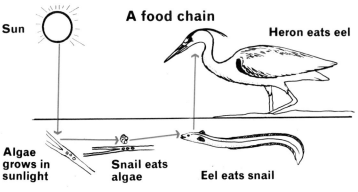

Sun

Algae grows in sunlight

Snail eats algae

Eel eats snail

Heron eats eel

Nuthatch

Beak short and thick for hammering open nuts

Hawfinch

Beak short and stumpy for cracking seeds

Swallow

Wide mouth for catching flying insects

Pied wagtail

Thin beak for picking up insects

Beak shapes

A bird's beak, or *bill*, is often a clue to the type of food it eats, and to the way it feeds. The illustrations show some examples of different beaks. What other birds have beaks like the ones shown here?

When you visit a zoo, look at the exotic beak shapes of foreign birds. Are these a pointer to any special food the birds eat?

Birds and berries

Make lists of the birds you see eating berries. Autumn and early winter are the best times for doing this. Good trees and shrubs to watch include elder, hawthorn, yew, blackberry, cotoneaster, rowan, holly and crab apple.

You can draw up a 'league table' to show the berried plants that attract the most species of birds, and the months when the birds are eating the berries.

If you can clearly see a bird eating berries, count the number it eats. Collect a few of the berries afterwards and weigh them. Then you can calculate the amount of food the bird ate at that meal.

A house sparrow's diet

Watch sparrows feeding near your home over the period of a month. Each time a group (or even just one bird) feeds on a particular type of food, mark this down as one *feeding record*.

See what different types of

food are being eaten. You can either record these under general headings (e.g. bird table foods; poultry foods; refuse; cereals; grains; berries), or be more specific and identify each food as accurately as you can (e.g. barley grains; elder berries).

After a month, you can add up the total number of feeding records for each type of food and can set out your results as a *histogram* (see page 55), or as a pie diagram.

Making a pie diagram

For this you will need to work out the totals of the feeding records for each type of food as a *percentage* of the total number of all the feeding records.

Draw a circle with a pair of compasses. The 360° of the circle represent the total (100 per cent) of all the feeding records. You then have to multiply the percentage of each type of food by 3.6.

For example, if 15 per cent of all the feeding records were of peas, multiply the 15 by 3.6. This will give you an answer of 54, so 54° of the circle will represent peas eaten by the house sparrow. Now mark off a 54° section with a protractor, from the centre of the circle – this is a *segment*. Repeat with segments for the other foods eaten.

Shoveler

Beak has filters for sieving foods from water

Snipe

Long and sensitive beak for probing into mud for worms

Goosander

Beak has ridges for holding fish

Peregrine falcon

Beak sharp and hooked for tearing flesh

Song thrush

one species, but with a variety of shadings and colours.

If you know of a thrush's 'anvil', visit it once a week and collect all the broken shells. Count the numbers of snails and work out their colour patterns. You could plot your weekly results as a histogram.

Try to watch how the thrush carries the shell, breaks it, pulls out the soft snail inside, wipes it on the ground and swallows it.

Try taking more records over other months. Do you think the diet of house sparrows changes from month to month? You can also record what foods other species prefer in the same way.

A song thrush's anvil
Song thrushes use stones, bricks and concrete paths to crack open the shells of snails (above). The snails are often of

Feeding patterns
Starlings often probe into areas of short grass on lawns and fields to find food. Watch one particular bird and time the number of *feeding probes* it makes in five minutes. Can you tell when it finds food? If you can see how many of the probes are successful, work

A starling's feeding pattern

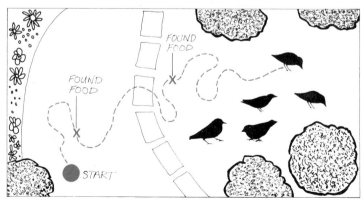

FOUND FOOD

FOUND FOOD

START

this number out as a percentage of the total number of probes the starling made.

Draw a map of a grassy area, like the one shown here, including any 'landmarks' like paths and large stones. On your map, plot the route a starling takes over a five minute period. Mark in the spots where it seemed to find food. What sort of *feeding route* did the bird take? Was it a twisting path like the one in this map? Work out from your map how far the starling walked in those five minutes.

You can study blackbirds in the same way.

Collecting pellets

Pellets are made up of undigested and compressed food, coughed up and ejected through a bird's mouth. They are usually oval in shape.

The pellets of gulls, herons, owls and hawks are all fairly obvious and easy to collect. Many common birds such as robins and blackbirds also produce pellets, but you will not find these so easily.

Gently pull the pellets apart in a shallow dish of water, and remove any items you recognize. The pellets of hawks and owls will contain bird feathers, bones and skulls; mammal fur, bones, skulls and teeth; and the hard wing

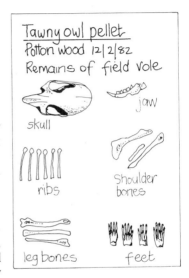

▲ A tawny owl's pellet and the bones found inside it.

cases of beetles. Gull pellets may have fishbones and heads; parts of crab and starfish; grass and cereal remains; as well as all sorts of rubbish like elastic bands, paper and string.

Stick all the items onto a piece of cardboard, with all similar items grouped together. Label the card with the name of the bird that produced the pellet, date and place found, and the contents.

5: Feeding Garden Birds

You can easily feed birds in your garden if you make artificial feeding stations and put out a variety of foods (see page 26). Do not put out food between April and July, as there is plenty of natural food available at this time.

Making a bird table

Find a piece of plywood at least 30 cm by 45 cm, suitable for outdoors. Fit narrow strips of wood to make a rim around the edges, but leave gaps at the corners. The rim will stop food being blown away and the gaps will drain rainwater.

Nail or bracket the bird table to a post about 1–1.5 metres high. Bang the post firmly into the ground to a depth of about 30 cm. Or, you could bracket the table to a wall or fence, or hang it from a tree branch. Make sure cats cannot easily get to it. A piece of wire netting round the post is a good way of preventing this (see the picture on the opposite page).

Put the table near a shrub or tree so the birds can use this as cover for their approach. It is also a good idea to put the table near a window, so you can watch it easily.

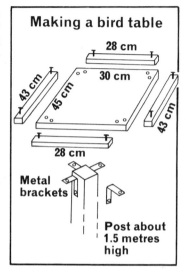

Making a bird table

28 cm

43 cm

45 cm

30 cm

43 cm

28 cm

Metal brackets

Post about 1.5 metres high

Other feeding equipment

Choose one or two of the following to go with your bird table.

Ground feeding tray: This is a large bird table top, about 60 cm × 90 cm, which lies flat on the ground.

Feeding log: Drill a small log of wood with some holes about 10–12 mm in diameter and 12–15 mm deep. Push foods like currants, sultanas and UNSALTED peanuts into the holes. Hang the log up with a metal screw-eye and string.

Scrap basket: Fold a piece of

▲ The following birds are feeding on the bird table, hanging tray, half coconut, string and bag of peanuts: male blackbird, blue tits, great tit, male greenfinch, house sparrow and robin. Can you identify them?

wire mesh about 30 cm × 20 cm into a cylinder and fasten it with small pieces of wire. The mesh holes should not be more than 0.5 cm in diameter. Wire two circular bits of mesh to the cylinder to make a bottom and an opening top lid. Make a firm wire handle and hang it from a branch, a bracket, or a hook on the bird table.

Coconut shells: These are very popular with tits. With help, you may be able to saw a coconut carefully in half – or just bang a hole in the shell, big enough for the tits to peck at the 'meat' inside it.

Some common garden birds

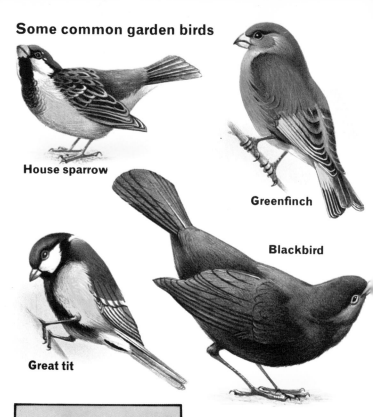

House sparrow

Greenfinch

Blackbird

Great tit

Suitable bird foods

Suitable foods for your bird table, ground feeding tray and scrap basket include stale bread, buns, cake, dried fruit (such as sultanas), peanuts, bacon rind, cheese and fruit. Birds will also eat most kitchen scraps that are not salty or spicy. You can also put out various seed mixtures.

Types of food seeds

Sunflower

Hemp

Teasle

Niger

Peanuts

HIGHEST NUMBER SEEN EACH DAY : JANUARY

DAY	1	2	3	4	5	6	7	8	9	10	11	12	13	14
H. Sparrow	20	25	15	12	16	10	12							
Greenfinch	1	–	4	7	4	3	2							
Blackbird	2	3	3	3	1	3	2							
Robin	1	1	2	1	1	2	1							
Starling	15	20	14	18	20	13	12							
B. Headed Gull	18	–	–	–	15	–	–							
Coal Tit	1	1	1	1	1	1	1							

Bird pudding: Shred a mixture of kitchen scraps, wild fruits and seeds into a bowl and stir melted fat (margarine, lard or dripping) over it – three parts of the mixture to one of fat. (BE CAREFUL NOT TO SCALD OR BURN YOURSELF WITH THE FAT!) When the 'pudding' has set, spoon it onto the bird table or ground tray.

Which birds visit your feeding stations?

Keep lists of the species that visit your feeding stations (see above). At what time of the year do you see the largest number of species? Does this coincide with cold weather, frosts or snow?

Which species feeds most often? Note down the number of times each species of bird feeds during one hour. Repeat during the same hour once a week.

Which is the favourite feeding station?

Put the same type of food (for example, bread or cheese) on the bird table, ground tray, or in the scrap basket. Note the species of birds that visit each one, and the number of visits made by each species. Do species have any preferences, either for type of feeding station or food?

Food preference tests

You can work out tests for yourself to see which foods are preferred by which birds. Here are a few ideas to start with:

Kitchen scraps: Choose four or five items (bread, cheese, cake, old fruit, bacon rind). Put approximately equal amounts of each on the bird table or ground tray. Note down the number of times different species of birds feed on each food item.

Commercial seeds: You can buy a wide variety of seeds from pet shops or corn merchants. Put small piles of these into jam jar lids and place on the bird table and/or the ground tray. Keep notes as before. Are the types of seed a bird prefers related to its type of beak?

Wild fruits and seeds: Collect some fruits and seeds in autumn, and store them in paper or muslin bags in a cool, dry place until you need them. Put out small quantities and record the species of birds that feed on them, as before. From this, you may discover the best foods to attract birds to your area.

How long do birds spend feeding?

If you can get hold of a *stopwatch,* record how long individual birds spend at your bird table. Compare the average times spent there by birds of various species.

Write down the number of common birds which feed at your bird table during ten minutes in each hour of daylight. It may be easiest to do this over one or two weeks. Do 'mealtimes' differ from one species to another? Does weather, or the season, affect the length of time, or the number of birds that feed at your bird table?

DOMINANT SPECIES AT THE TABLE

DOMINANT BIRD	BIRD IT CHASED	NO. OF TIMES
Robin	House Sparrow	6
House Sparrow	Robin	5
Starling	Robin	4
Greenfinch	House Sparrow	2
Starling	Greenfinch	3

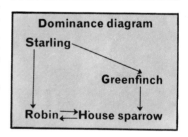

Dominance diagram

Starling → Greenfinch

Robin ⇄ House sparrow

Dominant species

Watch birds carefully to see which species are most *aggressive.* The chart above shows the sort of results you may get. You can then make your own 'Dominance diagram' like the one shown here.

The Bottle Test!

Blue and great tits often peck through foil milk bottle tops to get at the cream.

Different coloured tops (gold, silver)

Blue tit

Great tit

Fake foil top

Peanuts inside bottle

Beer bottle

Log covered with foil

Empty bottle with foil top

Milk bottle with no top

At different times, try putting out a variety of bottles or 'fake' bottles like those in the picture. Make silver foil tops for your bottles. Do tits strip the foil off the empty bottles? Does the colour of a painted bottle make any difference? Do the birds attack the foil on an empty beer bottle – or the foil on a log of wood? What happens to a bottle filled with unshelled peanuts?

Colour preferences

Use harmless *vegetable dyes* on bread, cheese or seeds to see if birds prefer the food they eat to be any special colour. Are naturally coloured foods most popular?

Hang up strings of dyed, unshelled peanuts from the bird table, or hang up shelled peanuts in differently coloured plastic mesh bags. What happens?

6: Secrets of Flight

A bird's greatest skill is being able to fly. This allows it to nest in inaccessible places and fly long distances to get food for its young. A swift may fly up to 800 kilometres a day to find food for its young. Migratory birds are able to fly from one part of the world to another.

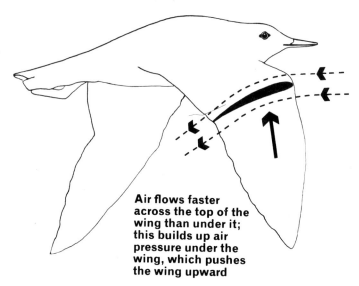

Air flows faster across the top of the wing than under it; this builds up air pressure under the wing, which pushes the wing upward

Demonstrating 'lift'

▶ If you hold a piece of paper close to your mouth and blow hard across the *top* of it, the paper will rise. In the same way, air passing over the curved top of a wing will 'lift' it, and the bird, in the air.

To fly, a bird has to both propel itself forward, and also stay up in the air. When it flaps its wings, the outermost *primary feathers* act as 'propellers' to push it along. The *flight feathers* give the bird the *lift* it needs to stay up in the air (see diagram, left).

Flight patterns

The drawings on the right show several kinds of flight patterns. Others you may see include:

Soaring over land: buzzard
Soaring over sea: fulmar
Soaring over cliffs: herring gull
Slow direct flight: heron

Keep a record of the different flight patterns you see.

Collecting wings

Cut off a wing from a dead bird at the first joint away from the shoulder. (REMEMBER TO WEAR GLOVES!) If there is any muscle showing, rub it with equal parts of *powdered alum* (from a chemist) and salt to preserve it.

Spread the wing out in the open position and pin it onto a piece of cardboard or flat wood. Keep it in a dry place until it sets firmly. You can then mount the wing on a piece of card or in a scrapbook. Fix it in position by glueing two strips of paper across the base and tip of the wing, and label it.

Flight patterns

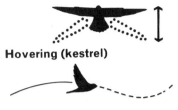

Hovering (kestrel)

Undulating flight – flap and glide (chaffinch)

Fast direct flight (starling)

Fast and twisting (swallow)

Acrobatic flight (lapwing)

Formation flying (geese)

Wing shapes and functions

► Long broad wings: birds that soar on thermals of hot air over land.

Buzzard

▼ Short broad wings for manoevrability.

Sparrowhawk

Manx shearwater

Peregrine falcon

◄ Long narrow pointed wings for high-speed flying.

▲ Long wings: birds that soar on air currents at sea or near cliffs.

Wing shapes

The shape of a bird's wing is closely related to the life it leads. It is possible to recognize at least four shapes, and these are shown on the opposite page.

Do you know the wing shapes of the following birds: swift, pheasant, stork, vulture, merlin, sparrow, magpie, pintail, fulmar, albatross, lesser black-backed gull, blue tit and swallow?

Making a flight mobile

Draw large-scale silhouette outlines of various birds in flight on thick white cardboard and cut them out (you could start by copying the shapes opposite). Paint the undersides in the birds' natural colours, or paint them all black. Attach the cut-outs with thread to different cross-pieces as shown in the picture.

You can make the cross-pieces from light wooden *doweling*. Then join the cross-pieces together with more thread. Or, you could simply hang your silhouettes from wire coathangers.

Wing speeds

Most small birds flap their wings too quickly for you to count, but larger ones, especially gulls, crows and herons, are easier. Use a stop-watch and count the number

A flight mobile

Cross-pieces

of wing flaps you see per second.

Slow-motion pictures show that some hummingbirds flap their wings at an amazing 50 times a second! See if you can work out the incredible number of wing flaps a hummingbird would make in six hours. Imagine the enormous amount of energy this requires; this is why hummingbirds feed on high energy foods, such as nectar.

Birds as flying machines

Birds and aircraft have some things in common and some differences, too. Compare the

33

▲ When taking off, a mallard 'jumps' from the water and flies up at a steep angle.

▲ A starling raises its wings and leaps from a perch to launch itself into the air.

two and see how many similarities and differences you can find. Things to consider include: streamlining, lightness and strength of body materials, steering mechanisms, take-off and landing methods, and wing shapes. What does a bird use for 'fuel' and 'engines'?

Take-off

Birds usually take off in one of three ways:

Running along the ground or water to build up speed.

Jumping directly into the air from ground or water.

Launching themselves into the air from perches.

Look at the methods of take-off for various species (especially starlings, finches, mallard, swans, moorhens, swallows, tits, herons and thrushes). Do any species use more than one method? Make sketches to show this. Do birds always take off *into* the wind? Does this help or hinder them?

A mute swan 'runs' across water to take off

In landing, it uses its feet and wings to 'brake'

Landing

A bird needs a good braking system to land gently. Mute swans stick out their webbed feet and 'water-ski' to a halt. Do all water birds land like this?

Watch a bird, such as a pigeon, coming in to land. Does it lose speed by gliding? At what height from the ground?

Does its tail help it to lose speed? Is its body vertical or horizontal? Does this help in braking?

Does a pigeon lose speed by flapping its wings to and fro? At what height? How does it use its legs and feet when landing? Do they absorb much 'shock' when they hit the ground?

Which action causes the pigeon to lose most of its speed? At what height from ground?

Some birds land on perches from above, losing speed like the pigeon. Other birds fly up to a perch from a lower level and lose speed in an upward glide.

Which landing method is used by the birds at your bird table? Do any species use both methods?

Speed of flight

Small birds usually fly between 30 and 60 km/h. Some larger birds fly between 60 and 100 km/h. Speeds can vary, though, depending on wind direction and method of flying. For example, a peregrine falcon has been timed at 280 km/h during a dive, but in normal flight it travels at about 80 km/h. Swallows can travel at about 160 km/h, but normally fly at about 50 km/h.

In one famous experiment a Manx shearwater was transported from its nest at Skokholm Island in South Wales and released in Boston, USA. It took only $12\frac{1}{2}$ days for the shearwater to return to its nest. Look at an atlas and work out the distance between South Wales and Boston. You can then work out what the average speed of this incredible journey was.

Measuring flight speeds

Use a stopwatch and time birds flying between any two points. You will have to estimate the distance between 'start' and 'finish'. Then you can calculate the average flight speed for different species.

Two people can measure the speed of birds flying to their *roosts* (see page 47). Stand 100–300 metres apart along a *flight line*. When the lead bird passes over you start the stopwatch and signal to your friend. When the bird flies over the second person,

▲ Homing pigeons are often transported hundreds of kilometres before being released to 'race' home.

he or she raises a hand and you stop the watch. Can you see if flight speeds are very different in calm or windy weather?

How fast does a homing pigeon fly?

The homing pigeon is a domestic variety of the wild rock dove, bred so that it will return to its home 'loft'. During both World Wars, many pigeons were used to carry secret messages across enemy lines.

If you can find someone who keeps pigeons they may help you find out how fast pigeons can fly by letting you time one of their birds. Check your watch with that of a friend and arrange for the pigeon to be released at a particular time, say ten kilometres away. One person should stay at the loft with the owner, and the other travel to release the bird.

You may need the owner's help to recognize 'your' particular bird when it returns to the loft. Note down its time of arrival and calculate the average speed of its journey. The fastest recorded speed for a homing pigeon appears to be about 140 km/h.

7 : Migration

A migrating bird will usually journey from its breeding area (after the breeding season) to other parts of the world, where it stays for the rest of the year.

Often whole populations migrate together. We are still not sure of some of the causes of migration, nor how birds find their way over such vast distances.

Migration is triggered off by the shortening of days in the autumn. Just before migration, birds may put on a lot of fat – the fuel that gives them the energy to fly thousands of kilometres.

Most migrating birds travel between 1000 and 1500 metres above the ground. They often fly to quite precise destinations, and seem to find their way by navigating from the positions of the Sun and other stars. Most small birds migrate at night, possibly because they are afraid of predators during the day. Swallows and hawks migrate in the day, and ducks, geese and gulls either by day or night.

▼ House martins and swallows gather in groups before leaving Europe to winter in Africa.

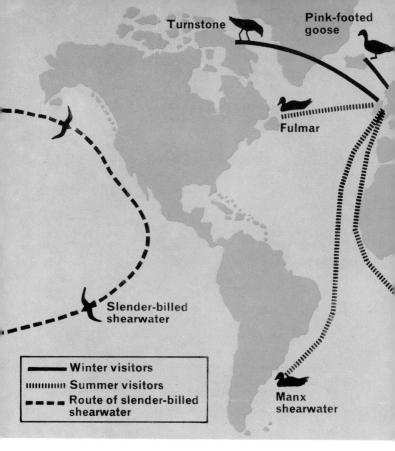

Turnstone

Pink-footed goose

Fulmar

Slender-billed shearwater

Manx shearwater

Winter visitors
Summer visitors
Route of slender-billed shearwater

About fifty species of birds which breed in northern Europe stay for the summer only. Mostly, they spend the winter in Africa where the weather is warmer, there is more food, and a longer day in which to collect it. In the same way, birds that breed in far northern or eastern areas, near to or even above the Arctic Circle, fly south to Europe for the winter.

How far do birds travel?
The approximate routes of some migrant birds are shown on the map above. Use the map scale to measure the distances they travel. Remember that, for all except the slender-billed shearwater, the distance migrated is the number of kilometres from the summer area to the wintering area *and back again*. Copy the

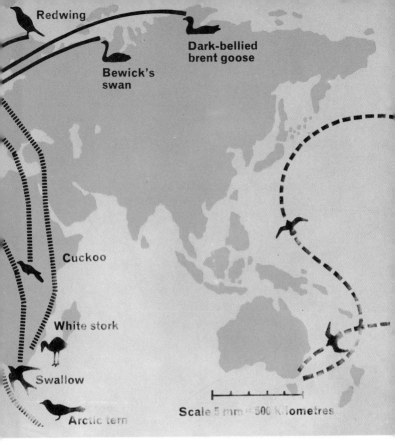

BIRD	DISTANCE	BIRD	DISTANCE
1		7	
2		8	
3		9	
4		10	
5		11	
6		12	

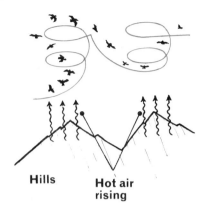

Hills **Hot air rising**

▲ Buzzards ride upwards on hot air thermals. They glide on their long broad wings from the top of one thermal until they find another one.

chart on the previous page into your notebook to record the distances travelled.

Most migrating land birds try to avoid crossing deserts, large areas of water, and mountains. They cross the Mediterranean Sea, for example, along the 'land bridges' at Gibraltar, Italy and the Bosphorus. This is especially necessary for storks, because they travel from one *thermal* to another on their broad wings. Thermals (see above) are currents of warm air, found only over land. Storks take three to four months to fly from Europe to South Africa, whereas fast-flying swallows take only two months.

The Arctic tern can journey to the very edge of Antarctica and back. A *ringed* bird, which bred on the Farne Islands in northern England, was found to be 27 years old! What an incredible distance it must have travelled over its lifetime if it migrated every year to the position shown on the map. How many kilometres do you think this was?

The swans and geese that winter in Britain travel in family parties, and the parents' experience helps them to lead their young to the best feeding areas.

Ocean wanderers like fulmars and Manx shearwaters cover vast distances, and the annual journey of the slender-billed shearwater around the Pacific Ocean is one of the longest migrations known.

Arrival and departure dates

It is fun to keep a weekly register of winter and summer migrants. *Summer visitors* may include swallows, swifts, house martins, spotted flycatchers and many species of warbler. *Winter visitors* could include redwings, fieldfares and bramblings, and many species of *wildfowl* (ducks, geese and swans). Make a list of the birds you see and put a tick alongside each one for every week that it spends in your area.

8 : Counting Birds

Flocks of birds that move fast, and where individuals are constantly changing place with each other, are a real challenge to count. Here is an easy and quick method of estimating numbers. With a bit of practice you can become quite good at it.

Look at the flock of birds in the picture above. Roughly twenty birds have been counted and a circle drawn around the space they occupy. If you imagine five such circles, you will get an estimate of 100 birds. Go on mentally dividing the flock into 20's or 100's until you have counted the whole flock.

It's fun to have a counting competition with your friends. Get someone to hold up a large number of dots on a piece of cardboard. Let everyone see the dots for thirty seconds and ask them to count in 20's and 100's. Then compare their answers to the real number.

The answers may vary a lot at first, but after five or six different exercises they should be more consistent.

You can also try estimating the number of people in a crowd. Check your estimate of a football, theatre or cinema crowd by multiplying the number of seat rows by the number of people in one row.

Counting exercises

You can practise estimating large numbers of things by looking at photographs. Start with fairly simple ones and then work up. Here are some examples for you to try. You could also throw handfuls of rice grains, bird seed or gravel onto a tray and practise on those.

▲ How many eggs?

▲ How many cars?

▲ How many people?

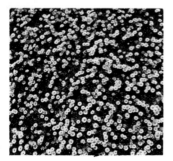

▲ How many flowers?

▲ How many birds?

Counting birds in the open

Estimate the size of any flock of birds you see, either flying overhead or stationary. Flocks on the ground are usually fairly well spaced out, but gulls following a plough may be constantly shifting. Look carefully to see if the flock contains more than one species.

You may have to count a flock a number of times before you get what you think is a good estimate, but practise as often as you can and you will soon find it quite easy.

Making monthly counts

If you can, visit a local water area once a month for a number of months and count or estimate the number of different *waterfowl* you see. Keep your records on a large chart with a histogram for each species. Add new columns to your histograms after each monthly count.

If you manage to persevere for a whole year you may notice that the numbers of some species have fluctuated. Are the highest numbers in spring and autumn when *birds of passage* stay for a short while? Are the numbers in winter higher than in summer? Do all the birds that remain in the summer breed?

You can also keep monthly counts of species on playing fields, pastures, arable fields and estuaries.

How many feathers on a bird?

Pluck a dead chicken and individually count the large feathers of its wings and tail. Mix the remaining feathers gently into a pile and divide into two smaller piles. Keep on dividing the piles in two until you get a pile of feathers you think you can count (see diagram below).

Work out what fraction this pile is of the whole. Count each feather in this pile and multiply the number by the fraction, i.e. if the pile is $\frac{1}{8}$th you multiply by 8. Don't forget to add on the wing and tail feathers.

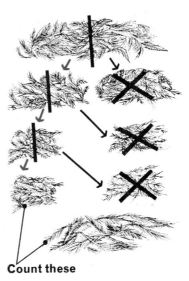

Count these

43

9: Taking a Census

Taking a *census* (population count) of the numbers of breeding birds in an area can be very difficult with such birds as warblers, or in habitats such as woods. The birds that are easiest are those that nest in very obvious *colonies*, like sand martins and herring gulls.

▼ Taking a population count of rooks in a rookery.

Other birds to try are those that make very obvious nests, such as house martins, carrion crows and magpies. Or, look for the birds themselves. Starlings and jackdaws perch near their *nest sites*, and waterfowl often lead their *broods* out into the open where you can easily count them. You can assume that each perching bird, or pair of birds, has a nest nearby. Some types of nest are shown on page 57. BE VERY CAREFUL NOT TO GO TOO CLOSE, OR DISTURB NESTING BIRDS.

Rooks

As shown in the picture, rook nests are easy to spot. Count the nests in use at the beginning of April. Try to find out how many rookeries are in your district, and see what trees are used. Is one type used more

44

supply of water? There may be several colonies along a suitable river. How far is each colony from another?

House martins
These birds build their nests of mud under the eaves (the edge of the roof) of houses. In which direction does the building face (e.g. north or south)? Do the birds choose any particular type of building (house, bungalow, etc.)?

Starlings and jackdaws
In towns, starlings often nest under the eaves of buildings, and the male may sing from vantage points such as television aerials. Assume each singing bird in April and May is one of a breeding pair. How many pairs are present in a half kilometre of street (one kilometre of houses)? Jackdaws may nest in chimneys.

than another? Rooks used to prefer elm trees, but millions of elms have now died from Dutch elm disease.

Sand martins
Sand martins nest in colonies along river banks or the sides of gravel or sand pits. They dig out nest holes about a metre deep. Count the number of holes in use at each colony? Are the colonies all near a

Waterfowl
Male ducks in June are usually a clue to the number of pairs breeding in the area. Counting females with broods also points to the numbers that have nested successfully. Do male mallards help rear the young as coots and moorhens do? Coot and moorhen parents often divide the brood between them, and you should allow for this when counting.

10: Roosting

Most birds *roost* (sleep or rest) at night because they feed during the day, but some night-hunters, like barn owls and tawny owls, spend the day roosting. Waders, such as oystercatchers, which feed on the seashore or in estuaries, roost at high tide when the mud or sand is too deeply flooded for them to feed.

Some species gather together to roost in flocks, while other birds roost on their own. Birds like house sparrows usually roost close to their feeding areas, but gulls and starlings may fly 30 kilometres or more to roost.

Roosting places

Birds usually roost in places that give them warmth, shelter and cover from predators. In towns, birds often choose trees near to street lamps for extra warmth. Some ground birds, such as pheasants, also roost in trees, away from predators. Lapwings roost in quite large flocks in the open where they can easily escape predators, and swifts can even roost while flying.

Some roosting sites are shown below. Also look on the ground, on ledges, in holes in walls and trees, and nest-boxes.

Roosting sites

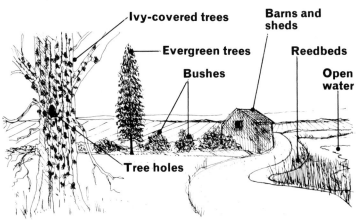

Ivy-covered trees

Barns and sheds

Evergreen trees

Reedbeds

Bushes

Open water

Tree holes

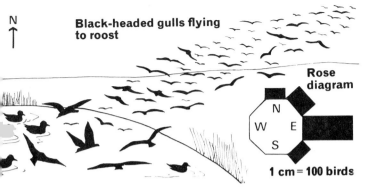

Black-headed gulls flying to roost

Rose diagram

N
W E
S

1 cm = 100 birds

Tracking down a roost

You may spot birds at dusk flying directly into roosts in conifer plantations or rhododendron bushes, for example. Or, look for 'whitewash' droppings under trees or ledges.

Be prepared to do a bit of travelling if you want to locate the roosts of the flocks you see flying overhead on winter afternoons. Gulls, starlings, wood pigeons and rooks are the easiest to follow.

Note down the flock's *direction of flight* on an Ordnance Survey map with an arrow, and the time. The end of the arrow should stop at the spot on the map where the flock disappeared from sight. Look for birds again at this place on the same, or another, afternoon at about the same time. Eventually you should find where their flight lines end.

Once you have found a roost try counting the birds as they fly into it (see pages 41–43),

▲ How to plot the direction of arrivals at a roost. The numbers of gulls from north, north-east, east and south-east are shown on a rose diagram.

and make a histogram. The vertical axis of the histogram should be the numbers of birds, and the horizontal axis should be split into 15 minute periods.

Plotting the direction of incoming birds

You may need the help of a friend for this. Using a compass, one of you should work out the direction from which each group of birds arrives at the roost. The other person notes this down, together with an estimate of the number of birds in each group.

Add up all the numbers for the birds that arrived from each different direction (north, north-east, etc.) and make a *rose diagram* (see picture above).

47

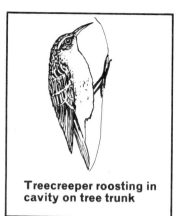

Treecreeper roosting in cavity on tree trunk

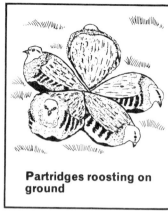

Partridges roosting on ground

You should then see clearly the direction from which most of the roosting birds come. If most birds arrive from one direction, is this due to any special land feature, such as a river which the birds follow?

How birds roost

Some species roost with their heads resting on their backs; others hunch up. Some birds, like woodpeckers and tree-creepers, cling vertically to tree trunks. Gulls and water-fowl usually roost on water. What positions do pigeons, doves and starlings use when roosting?

Partridges roost on the ground in a circle with all the birds facing outwards. How would this help if they were disturbed by a fox?

How do roosting birds stay on their perches?

When you examine a dead bird, straighten its leg and you will see that the toes also become straight and rigid. Bend the leg back towards the body and watch the toes curl inwards. This is how the bird roosts on a perch. When it lands and bends its legs, the toes curl round the perch and grip it tightly, even when the bird is asleep.

▲ Leg of a perching bird. When the leg is bent, the tendon (in black) is stretched, and the toes curl around the perch.

11 : Territories

A bird's *territory* is the area it defends against other birds of the same species. Male birds usually set up territories in the breeding season, and defend them by singing (often from a song post) and displaying.

For birds like the robin, the territory has to be big enough to provide food for both parents and young. Because breeding pairs of robins defend their territories they are fairly well spread out.

The birds get to know 'their' area very well. They learn the best places to feed, drink, bathe and roost. They also know the best spots of cover when escaping from a predator. A robin's territory may be about a hectare, a tawny owl's is about eight hectares, and a golden eagle's as much as 60 sq km.

Rooks and house martins fly quite a distance from their nests to look for food. So although they do defend their territory, it may be as small as a few square metres. These birds require space only for a nest and for rearing their young, as they can find food over a large area without needing to defend it.

▼ Map showing the territories of two pairs of blackbirds.
Symbols: **D** – displaying male;
S – song post/singing bird;
X – sighting of a blackbird.

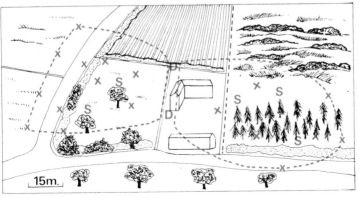

Types of song post

Skylark: in mid air/sky
Reed bunting: fence post

Starling: washing line
Song thrush: small branch

Little owl: tree stump
Wren: undergrowth

Plotting a blackbird's territory

Get a large-scale Ordnance Survey map, or make your own sketch map, of an area where you know there are blackbirds in the spring. You can also plot a robin's territory in the same way.

When you spot the bird, mark its position on the map with a cross (**X**). If the bird flies to another part of the same area put another cross on the map. If a male bird is singing, add the symbol **S**.

The mapping of these song posts is valuable because they are often in a central or prominant part of the bird's territory.

You may hear another blackbird (or robin) singing some way off at the same time. Mark its position if you can. When you see two males together, this may be a clue to the edges of each of their territories.

If the birds are displaying, mark the map with the symbol **D**. Two males will often hop along parallel to one another but a few metres apart, and pause for a long time. There may even be a brief confrontation before one bird is chased off.

When you think you have enough information, draw a line around the outermost crosses or other symbols on the map. The area within your line will be approximately each bird's territory. Can you work out how to calculate the area of the territory?

Coot and moorhen territories
Coots and moorhens usually breed on rivers, ponds or lakes, and their territories may also include pieces of shore. You can easily watch both species. Their songs are only short croaks, and you may notice that they display and fight more than songbirds do.

Use similar methods and symbols to plot their territories as before. Do coots have larger areas of water in their territories than moorhens?

Recognizing song posts
Song posts are often very conspicuous, and some are shown in the drawings opposite. Make a list of the types of song posts in your area, and the birds using them. In built-up areas, birds may use buildings, chimneys, walls, telegraph wires and poles as song posts, and in the country tall trees, shrubs, gates and fences. Make sketches of song posts you have seen, and the birds using them.

Also, look out for birds from one species (starling or blackbird, say), and see which type of song post they use in various habitats (towns, parks,

▼ How to measure the height of a song post.

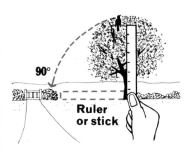

gardens and woods). How many song posts are man-made?

Height of song posts
The drawing above shows you how to estimate the height of a song post (or anything else for that matter). Stand quite a way away from the song post. Hold a ruler or a stick straight up in front of you and line up the top of the ruler with the bird. Move your thumb down the ruler until it aligns with the bottom of the song post.

Keep this measurement on the foot of the post, and turn the ruler 90°. Note the spot on the ground that now lines up with the end of the ruler (a hedge, for example). Go over to that spot and pace out the distance between this point and the base of the song post. Measure your average pace, so you can calculate the distance. This measurement is also the approximate height of the song post.

Testing a territory

Put a model of a robin into another robin's territory in spring and watch the 'owner' trying to drive the intruder out. You can make the model from *papier mâché*, or use a red apple or one half of a potato painted red. Alternatively, you can prop a mirror up on a lawn with some food in front of it. The feeding robin will then be reflected in the mirror.

When the bird spots its reflection or the model, watch how it behaves. It may sing or display to it; fly towards or away from it; or even attack it. The 'owner' robin will often puff out its red breast and arch its beak and head over its back.

Remember that the model robin (or the mirror reflection) will not go away as a normal robin 'intruder' would. So ONLY USE IT FOR A FEW MINUTES AT A TIME, so that you don't drive off the resident robin.

Individual spacing

Each bird also defends a small area around itself, often only a few centimetres, sometimes a few metres. Within this area, the bird will not tolerate the presence of another bird of its own species. *Ornithologists* call this the *'least individual distance'*. You can easily see this behaviour in winter when many birds feed in flocks.

Feeding distances

Put two dishes of food at opposite ends of your bird table (see picture opposite). What happens when two birds of the same species come to feed? If they feed together happily, move the food dishes a little closer to each other. Keep doing this until two birds of the same species will not feed without squabbling or one being forced to leave.

This distance of the dishes is approximately the least individual distance tolerated by that pair of birds. Watch other species of birds and you will soon see if they also need the same distance.

A ruler fixed to the edge of the bird table will help you to check the distances more accurately.

To help you measure a space between birds feeding on the ground, lay down a long piece of string with bits of cord or material tied on it at 20 cm intervals. Place the food alongside the string as before.

Do this experiment as often as you can, especially with house sparrows, starlings, pigeons, finches, tits and

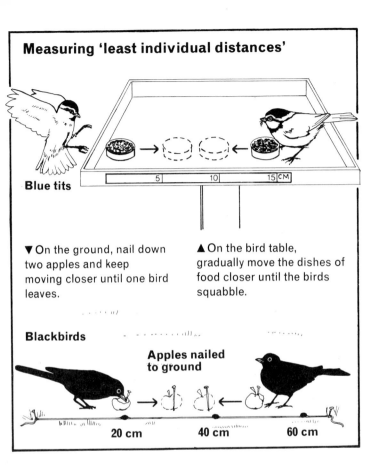

Measuring 'least individual distances'

Blue tits

▼ On the ground, nail down two apples and keep moving closer until one bird leaves.

▲ On the bird table, gradually move the dishes of food closer until the birds squabble.

Blackbirds

Apples nailed to ground

20 cm   40 cm   60 cm

thrushes, and compare the average distances for different species.

Feeding in flocks
Birds like rooks, black-headed gulls and fieldfares feed together in flocks on farmland and playing fields. Ducks and coots feed on ponds and reservoirs in winter. You will see how each bird spaces itself out within the flock, probably so it can gather food without too much competition from its neighbours.

Estimate the distance between individual birds in a flock. Make about 20 records for each species, work out the average distances and compare them with those of other species.

12 : Reproduction

Many small birds pair up for one year only, but long-lived birds, like mute swans and kittiwakes, normally pair up for life. It is usually the male bird who sets up a territory and attracts a female by singing, or displaying.

After mating, the female lays her eggs, usually in a nest, and *incubates* them until they hatch.

Structure of an egg

Look at a chicken's egg. The hard *shell* protects the contents from minor knocks, and helps to keep them at a fairly even temperature.

If possible, look at the outside of the eggshell through a hand lens. First, wipe some black boot polish on the shell. Can you see any small holes or *pores*? These let fresh air pass into the egg, and used air, containing carbon dioxide, pass out. Are there more pores near the blunt end of the egg?

Crack open the egg and look at the contents in a saucer. There will be a small spot on the *yolk*. In a *fertilized egg* this *germinal disc* would have developed into the chick. The two twisted strands called *chalazae*,

A developing egg

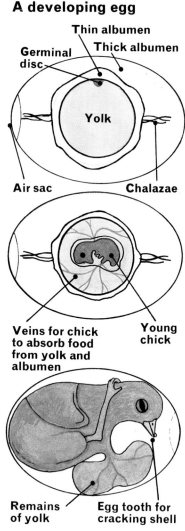

Thin albumen
Thick albumen
Germinal disc
Yolk
Air sac
Chalazae

Veins for chick to absorb food from yolk and albumen
Young chick

Remains of yolk
Egg tooth for cracking shell

54

attached one on each side of the yolk, ensure the germinal disc is always on top of the yolk.

The egg 'white' (*albumen*) and yolk between them provide food, water, vitamins and minerals for the developing chick. Two thin *membranes* separate the shell from the albumen. At the blunt end of the egg there is an *air space*, used to supply the chick.

Egg shapes

Each species usually lays eggs of the same shape. Use some modelling clay to copy the egg shapes of the guillemot and herring gull shown below. (You can find other egg shapes in some guide books, but you must NEVER COLLECT WILD BIRDS' EGGS.) Place both your models on a large tray and tip the tray up about one centimetre at one end. What happens

Histogram

▲ Make a histogram of how much time a bird spends singing. Choose a common bird, like a blackbird or song thrush, which is setting up a nesting territory and singing a lot to attract a mate. Use a stopwatch to time how many minutes in an hour the bird sings. Then use your records to make up a histogram like the one above.

▼ A guillemot egg is 8 cm long and 5 cm wide. The widest part is 3 cm from the blunt end.

▲ A herring gull egg is 7 cm long and 5 cm wide. It is widest near the middle.

▲ The ringed plover's eggs are similar in colour to the rocks or gravel on which they are laid.

▲ Lapwings lay their eggs in grassy places. Note how the eggs and chick are coloured.

to the eggs when they roll down the tray? In real life, both eggs are laid on cliff ledges, but the herring gull needs a nest. Can you see why?

Camouflaged eggs

Eggs have different colours and markings to hide them from predators, but the eggs of birds like owls, which are hidden in holes, tend to be white.

Try this test. Paint a chicken's egg with the same colours and markings as a ringed plover's egg (you can look up the colour details in a guide book). When the egg is dry, put it in a sandy area like a long-jump pit. Put an ordinary white chicken's egg about two or three metres away from it.

Now ask a friend to walk towards the sand pit. At what

distance does your friend see both eggs? Now do the same test with a fake lapwing egg on a bare patch of lawn.

Nests

Most birds build actual nests, but some just lay their eggs on bare ground. The following are some natural *nest sites* chosen by birds:

Excavated tree holes: willow tit
Natural tree holes: blue tit
Cliff ledges: kittiwake
Old rabbit burrows: wheatear
Tops of trees: buzzard
Bushes: blackbird
On the ground: lapwing
Floating on water: coot
Tussocks: snipe

We provide good artificial nesting sites for many species of birds with our houses, sheds, factories, walls and machinery, and by leaving litter around.

Note down the species you see using such artificial sites.

Collecting old nests

Winter is the time to collect old nests. DO MAKE SURE THE NEST IS NOT BEING USED. Make a note of a nest being used in the breeding season, and identify its owner, so you can find it again when breeding has finished.

Whenever you remove an old nest from a tree or bush, be careful not to damage the plant. DO NOT COLLECT NESTS FROM HOLES, as you may damage the hole and it could be needed again next year. NOR COLLECT REALLY BIG NESTS (heron or buzzard, for example), as the same birds may want to use them next year.

You should be able to collect at least four types of nests:
Cup-shaped nest: blackbird or chaffinch
Domed nest: wren or long-tailed tit
Flat nest: bullfinch or wood pigeon
Ground nest: pheasant or mallard

Different types of nest

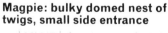

Wood pigeon: flimsy platform of twigs

Sandwich tern: eggs on bare ground, part of nesting colony

Magpie: bulky domed nest of twigs, small side entrance

Kingfisher: hole in river bank

57

If the nest is damp, dry it out near a fire or radiator. Make a label with the species, date you found it, height from the ground, habitat, and plant the nest was in. Display your nests on a table, or store them in cardboard boxes.

What is a nest made of? Carefully take an old nest to pieces (especially a house sparrow's or blackbird's) to see the different types of *nesting materials* (leaves, straw, moss, paper and so on) it is made of. Stick samples of these materials onto cardboard for display.

Making a nestbox
Many hole- and cavity-nesting birds, like tits, will nest in nestboxes. The diagram opposite illustrates how you can make a nestbox from a single plank of wood.

During the winter, nail the nestbox to a tree, shed or wall, about two metres off the ground and sheltered from the rain and sun. (It is best if the entrance faces north-east). If you put up about three boxes in an area of about half a hectare, with luck a pair of birds should nest in at least one of them. IF YOUR NESTBOX IS USED, TRY NOT TO LOOK INTO IT TOO OFTEN. LOOK IN BRIEFLY ONCE OR TWICE A WEEK WHEN THE PARENT BIRDS ARE AWAY.

If you put out some nesting materials the birds will often use them. Cut up some materials, such as coloured string or wool, into two- or three-centimetre strips. Tie them into loose bundles and hang near the nestbox.

Recording nest details
You can record a lot of interesting facts about the birds that use your nestbox.

Write down the dates when you saw the birds carrying nest materials. Were any of these the materials you put out? How many visits an hour did the birds make with nesting materials?

On which dates did you first see eggs? How many eggs were laid?

Note the dates when the parents start to bring food to the nest. This shows that the eggs have hatched. Where do the parents get food? How far from the nest do they have to fly for it? What kind of food do they bring to their nestlings? How many visits do the parents make in an hour with food for their young?

Work out a diagram to show the dates when you observed the birds gathering nest material, laying, incubating, and feeding the young.

If you are lucky enough to have blue or great tits nesting

Making a nestbox

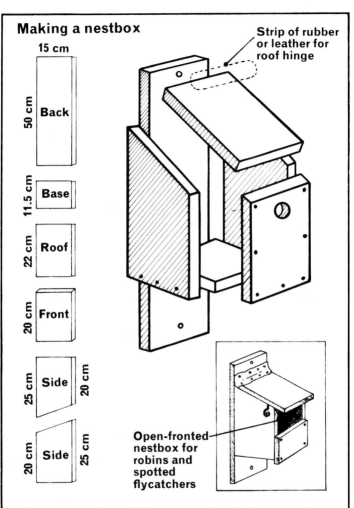

Strip of rubber or leather for roof hinge

15 cm

50 cm — **Back**

11.5 cm — **Base**

22 cm — **Roof**

20 cm — **Front**

25 cm | 20 cm — **Side**

20 cm | 25 cm — **Side**

Open-fronted nestbox for robins and spotted flycatchers

▲ Saw a plank of wood into pieces as shown here. Cut the tops of the side pieces at an angle so the roof will slope downward and the rain will drain off. Cut an entrance hole 3 cm in diameter. This will let in great and blue tits, but keep out starlings. The entrance to an open-fronted box should be 10 cm high. Nail the pieces together.

Blue tit

1 day old

3 weeks old

▲ At one day old the blue tit is helpless. At 3 weeks, it is starting to feed by itself.

Pheasant

1 day old

3 weeks old

▲ A pheasant chick is able to feed itself at one day old and is well grown at 3 weeks.

in your nestbox, these are wonderful species to watch.

Young birds

The eggs of most small birds are incubated for about two weeks before hatching. Larger birds, such as mallard, may incubate their eggs for three to four weeks.

The young of many ground-nesting birds leave the nests within hours of hatching and are called *nidifugous* ('nest fugitives'). The young of most song birds remain in the nest for over two weeks and are called *nidicolous* ('nest dwellers').

If you can, using binoculars and keeping your distance so you do not disturb the birds, look at the chicks of different species of birds and try to compare them.

Is each chick naked or covered in down?

Are its eyes closed or open?

Can it run about or does it remain helpless at the nest?

Is it camouflaged in any way?

Does it feed on its own, or does it have to be fed by its parents?

The picture above shows blue tit and pheasant chicks at different stages of their growth. How do your answers to the questions above help you to appreciate the differences between them?

Why should the chicks of ground-nesting birds be so well developed and independent so soon after hatching?

13: Habitats

A bird's habitat is the type of country or area where it lives. Some examples of habitats, split into three broad groups, are shown below.

Choose three different types of habitat, one from each list, and visit each one for an equal length of time, for one or two hours each, for example.

Identify and make a note of every species you see and hear (a field guide will help you identify the species). It is best not to record birds that are just flying over an area without

▼ *Water areas:*
Rivers
Reservoirs
Lakes and
  lochs
Ponds
Flooded
  gravel pits
Marshes
Bogs
Old sewage
  farms
Open sea
Estuaries

▼ *Land with few trees:*
Moors
Heaths
Mountain tops
Sea cliffs
Seashore
Quarries
Derelict land
Agricultural land
Lawns and playing
  fields
Rubbish dumps
Built-up areas
Many suburban
  gardens

▼ *Land with many
  trees:*
Deciduous woods
Coniferous woods
  and plantations
Parkland
Orchards
Some churchyards
Some old country
  gardens
Old hedges

landing, as they may not belong to that area.

As you become more expert, start counting the numbers of each species that you see.

When you have a list for each habitat, compare the species you saw. You may discover that some species are found just in one type of habitat, while others are in more than one. You may see, for example, that jays and bullfinches keep to areas with many trees; that skylarks and reed buntings keep to areas with few trees, and coots and moorhens keep to water areas. But you may regularly see other birds, such as starlings and greenfinches, in all three habitats.

Birds in similar habitats

Now choose three similar habitats from *one* of the lists on page 61. Note down the birds you see in each habitat.

You may spot quite a lot of species. The following examples will give you some idea of the habitats you can

◄ The following woodland birds are in this picture: carrion crow, wood pigeon, tawny owl, chiffchaff, bullfinch, tree sparrow, nuthatch, blackbirds (male and female), green woodpecker. How many can you identify?

choose and the different birds you will find in them:

Land with many trees – deciduous woods, coniferous woods, hedgerows: You will find coal tits and goldcrests mostly in coniferous woods, with blue tits and green woodpeckers in deciduous woods. You will see many, but not all, woodland birds in the hedgerows because these are really strips of woodland. See if you can find any birds in hedgerows that are not in the two types of woodland?

Land with few trees – built-up areas, agricultural land, derelict land: You should see *game birds*, like pheasants and partridges on agricultural land, especially where cereals are grown. Finches, including linnets and goldfinches, are common on derelict land where there are lots of weed seeds to eat. You should see starlings and house sparrows in all three habitats.

Water areas – rivers, reservoirs, estuaries: Kingfishers and grey wagtails are normally seen along rivers; coots and tufted ducks on reservoirs, and shelduck and cormorants on estuaries. You should see blackheaded gulls and mallard in all three habitats.

Field birds

Red-legged partridge

Pheasant (female)

Lapwing

Fieldfare

Rook

Skylark

Neighbouring habitats
Note down the species of birds you see in habitats which are next door to each other. Examples are:
Open sea – seashore – sea cliffs.
Fields – hedges – woods.
Open water – marsh – woods.
Built-up areas – town parks – ponds.

Cultivated land areas
The appearance of cultivated land changes dramatically over the year (think of lawns and hayfields before and after they are mown, and arable fields and vegetable gardens before and after the crops are harvested).

Find an area of land that is going to be ploughed, or dug up on a certain day. Make a list of the species of birds and the numbers you see there on a day *before* the change happens, on the day it is *being* cultivated, and again *one week later*.

On which day are there most species of birds and in the greatest numbers? Is there more food available when the ground is being turned over? Look at the ground, and see how many foods you can find, such as earthworms, 'leather jackets' (cranefly larvae), and other insect larvae.

Seasonal differences
Go to any of the habitats at different times of the year and record the species and numbers of birds you see. In summer you may spot some birds like swallows that will have migrated by the winter. In winter you may find such visitors as redwings and fieldfares.

Ecological niches

Different species which use different parts of a habitat to live and feed are said to be occupying different *ecological niches*.

Visit a deciduous wood for two hours and record the 'niche' (tree layer, woody parts – trunks and branches, shrub layer, field layer, or ground layer) of every bird you identify (some niches are shown in the picture on page 62).

Write down the birds you see most often in each of the five niches. In winter, for example, blue tits are usually on small branches; treecreepers are on trunks; robins are in the shrub layer; wrens in the field layer, and blackbirds on the ground layer.

Compare the ecological niches of the same species in summer and winter. Winter will probably show you the birds' *feeding niches* only, but in summer, if you make a note of singing birds, you may also discover their *reproductive niches*.

Waterbirds

Divide a lake or pond into sections and work out the ecological niches (open water, reed swamp, marsh, or dry land) of the birds you see – these will usually be their feeding niches. Some species of birds you are likely to see are shown in their feeding niches in the picture below.

Single species

Choose a single species of bird and observe it regularly over a year. Make a record of all the information you can discover about its habitat (or habitats).

▼ Feeding niches of waterbirds, which range from wigeon feeding on land to tufted duck, which dives in deep water.

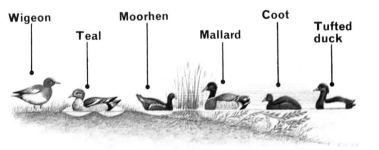

Wigeon

Teal

Moorhen

Mallard

Coot

Tufted duck

14: Drinking

Animals, including birds, need water to help digest their food and carry it around the body. Muscles contain a lot of water needed to convert food into energy to run and fly. So, if there were no water to drink animals' bodies would not be able to work efficiently and they would die.

Birds lose *water vapour* from their lungs and air sacs when they breathe out. They also lose *liquid water* in their droppings. Unlike humans, birds do not have sweat glands, so they do not lose water by perspiring. However, on very hot days they pant, like dogs, and lose a greater amount of water.

Birds replace water loss in several ways. The most obvious way is by drinking, but some water also comes from fleshy fruits and berries.

Birds that spend most of their lives at sea drink salt-water, which would be harmful if they had not developed special glands for *desalinating* (removing the salt from) the seawater.

Making a bird pool

You can make a simple pool by digging a shallow hole in the

A simple pool

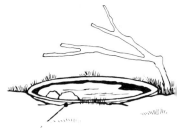

Dustbin lid sunk in ground

ground, and placing an old dustbin lid upside down in the hole, so that its rim is flush with the soil surface (above). Put a few large pebbles or bricks in it and fill it with water to a few centimetres from the top, so there are suitable *perching places* in the middle and on the edges for the birds to drink and bathe.

You can make a bigger pool by digging an area of one to two square metres and lining it with tough plastic (butyl sheeting. Make the deepest part about 10 cm, but most of it should be only 2 to 5 cm deep. As many sides as possible should slope gradually to the deepest part.

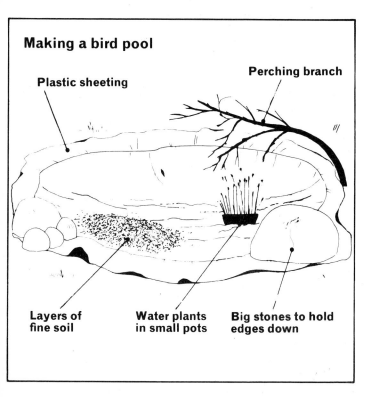

Making a bird pool

Plastic sheeting

Perching branch

Layers of fine soil

Water plants in small pots

Big stones to hold edges down

Remove any sharp stones before laying down the plastic sheet, making sure at least 10 cm on all sides lie on the undug ground around the edge of the hole. Cover this 10 cm wide 'apron' with earth and stones, or pieces of turf, to hold the sheet in place.

Sprinkle sand or fine soil to form a 2-cm thick layer over the bottom of the pool. Put a few larger stones, bricks or wooden perches in the deeper part of the pond. Fill up with

water, but remember to leave some very shallow edges. (In hot weather you may have to top up the pond occasionally because the heat will evaporate some of the water.) You can make the pond more attractive by planting some water plants in pots.

Drinking methods

Birds will start to drink at your pool as soon as there is water in it. Keep a checklist of the birds that visit it – you will be surprised how many there are.

You should see birds drinking in at least one of two ways. For example, a blackbird will put its beak in the water and then *lift* its head up, beak pointing to the sky, so water can trickle down its throat. A pigeon will keep its beak in the water and *suck* the water into its throat.

Make a list of the ways other birds drink and draw sketches of them. Swallows and martins quench their thirst by briefly *dipping* their wide bills into water while flying over it.

Think of all the liquids you drink in a day (milk, tea, coffee, soft drinks). Estimate the total volume in litres of the liquid you drink. Then assume that one litre weighs one kilogram and convert this volume into a weight. You can then calculate the amount of liquid you drink in a day as a percentage of your body weight.

Other animals

How does a cat or dog drink? Is there any difference between the ways they drink and those of a cow or horse? Insects have developed special ways of drinking their food. Butterflies have a coiled proboscis for drinking nectar. How do you think a housefly 'drinks' spilled sugar?

68

Dunnock

▲ A garden pool in use. Notice the two methods of drinking of the birds at this pool. The song thrush scoops water up into its beak, then holds its head up to let the water trickle down its throat, whereas the collared dove keeps its beak in the water and drinks by sucking the water into its throat. Notice, also, how the blackbird is bathing. Bathing methods are described in the next chapter.

Greenfinch (male)

Song thrush

Collared dove

Blackbird (male)

Water pollution

Since all animals and plants need water to live, it is very important that water is not polluted by harmful chemicals.

Industry uses a lot of water, and factories should purify (clean) it before returning it to a river or sea. The water used in our houses is purified at sewage farms.

Farmers spray chemicals, such as pesticides, herbicides and fertilizers, onto their crops and, unfortunately, large amounts get washed into the soil by rain and then drain into rivers and seas.

The pollution of water plants and waterbirds by agricultural chemicals is a very serious problem in some parts of the world. Oil spilt from ships that are damaged at sea also badly affect seabirds and other marine life.

15: Bathing

Birds usually bathe in one of three ways: in water, dust, or in the sun. Afterwards, they usually spend some time *oiling* and *preening*, to keep their feathers and skin clean, free from *parasites* (ticks, lice, fleas), and waterproof.

▲ Song thrush splashing in water.

▲ Mallard throwing water onto its back and wings.

Make a list of the different species of birds you see bathing in water. Which birds come most often, at what time of day and state of weather? How long do they bathe; in what depth of water; alone or in flocks? Is bathing 'catching' from one bird to another?

Ratio of drinking to bathing

Draw two columns marked 'Drinking' and 'Bathing', and tick the appropriate column for each species you see. After about 20 records for each species add up the ticks in each column and work out the ratio of drinking to bathing. Which does each species do most often?

How birds bathe

Birds most often bathe in water in one of three ways:

A bird like a mallard *floats* on the water, dipping its head and shoulders under, and throwing water onto its back and wings. The wings beat or flick on the water.

A bird like a blackbird *stands* in water and dips its head and throat. The bird flaps its wings up and down, *spraying* water onto its back and wings, and shakes its beak from side to side.

A few birds, like swallows, bathe while flying. They either *touch the surface* of the water with their bodies, or briefly *plunge in*.

Try to find out which methods of bathing different

▲ House sparrows dust bathing.

birds use, such as swifts, ducks, swans, terns, kingfishers, starlings, gulls and canaries.

How do birds dry themselves after bathing? Are the feathers *ruffled* in any way? Most garden birds ruffle their feathers and shake their bodies to get rid of excess water. Gulls sometimes shake their bodies in mid flight.

Dust bathing

You probably will not see birds dust bathing as often as bathing in water, and fewer species do this, too. House sparrows, skylarks and pheasants regularly dust bathe in fine sand or earth. Free-range chickens love taking dust baths. They work the dust into their feathers and then shake it out again. Ornithologists think the dust helps to dislodge the parasites that live among birds' feathers.

Making a sparrow dustbox

Make a shallow wooden box about 60 cm long, 30 cm wide and 8 cm high – or ask a greengrocer for an old tomato box. Fill the box half full with a mixture of fine dry earth and sand, and put it on the ground at a place where you often see house sparrows gathering (near a bird table is a good place).

Look at the ways in which the sparrows dust bathe. Do they bathe in small groups? Do they wallow in the dust? Describe or sketch the ways in which they use their beaks, feet, wings and bodies to work the dust into their feathers. Can you spot any movements similar to those used when they bathe in water?

Make a list of other birds which use your dustbox, either singly or in small flocks.

▲ A blackbird sunbathes with its wings and tail spread out.

Sunbathing

Birds often sunbathe on flat hard ground near to cover. Birds such as blackbirds may lie on the ground, tails fanned and wings completely outstretched. Their body feathers may be ruffled. In some cases, birds close their eyes and half open their beaks. We do not yet properly understand why birds sunbathe, but sun rays on the oils in the feathers does help make vitamin D.

Record the different species you see sunbathing. Make sketches of the different positions they use.

Preening and oiling

Preening and oiling are usually done together. Oil is made in the *preen gland* which is situated at the base of the tail (this gland is the 'parson's nose' of a chicken). A bird smears some oil on its beak and then spreads the oil through its feathers by preening. The bird sometimes rubs its head straight onto the oil gland, or scratches oil over its head with its foot.

As well as getting rid of dirt and parasites, oiling and preening keep the feathers in good condition. Preening re-arranges feathers and *rezips* the barbs of any bedraggled ones (see page 14).

Rezipping a feather

You can often find flight feathers under trees, and at roost sites. Unzip the barbs of a feather by stroking it the 'wrong' way (from tip to base). Now stroke the feather the right way (from base to tip) and you should be able to rezip the barbs. This is what a bird does when it preens a feather.

Collect as many different feathers as you can. Once you have rezipped your feathers you can mount and keep them.

Head scratching

There are two ways in which birds scratch their heads with their feet during preening:

Indirect scratching: the foot is brought up over the wing, which is sometimes lowered.

Direct scratching: the foot is brought up under or in front of the wing.

Preening postures

Knot

Black-headed gull

Note which method of scratching different species of birds use. Most song birds scratch indirectly, but many other groups of birds (including wildfowl and game birds) do so directly.

Do other animals bathe in water, dust bathe or sun-bathe, preen or groom themselves? If so, how?

Testing a preen gland for oil
Rub a piece of tissue paper onto a chicken's preen gland. Hold the paper up to the light. The oil should show up as a translucent spot.

Mounting feathers

▶ Push the end of the feather into a cork or piece of balsa wood. Or fix it to a piece of card with strips of glued paper, and label it.

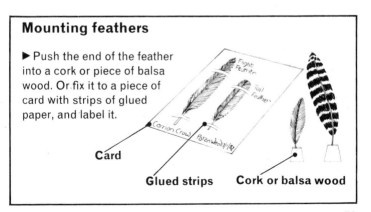

Flight Feather

Tail Feather

Carrion Crow   Palonwood 1/1/18

Card

Glued strips   **Cork or balsa wood**

16: Diving Birds

Waterfowl usually dive for food (fish near the surface of the water, water weeds, or underwater snails). They also dive to escape from enemies. When people or predators surprise a brood of water-birds, they all immediately dive and swim away in different directions.

Waterbirds usually dive in one of two ways: some *plunge* into the water from the air, and some *dive from a sitting position* on the water. Make a list of the species that you see diving. Which of these diving methods (or any others) do they use? Do they dive in sea-water or freshwater, or both? Some birds swim underwater by paddling their webbed feet, others use their wings as oars.

Timing dives

You should see a good selection of diving birds on lakes, reservoirs, gravel pits and town park ponds (BE CAREFUL NOT TO FALL IN!). Choose a bird a little apart from the rest. Start a stopwatch when the bird dives and stop it when the bird surfaces. Note down the time the bird spends underwater. Repeat for different birds of the same species. Work out and compare the time of the longest and shortest dives, and the average time for all the dives.

Repeat when the water conditions are different (calm or choppy). Do birds spend a longer or shorter time under choppy water? If so, why do you think this is?

When do birds dive?

Look at a flock of waterbirds every half hour and count the numbers diving. Estimate the number of birds in the flock and calculate what percentage of birds were diving in each half hour. Make a graph. One axis of the graph should be the hour of the day, and the other should be the percentages of birds diving.

You will then see the time of day when most birds are diving, and probably feeding. Are there any differences between species? For example, plant-feeders, such as coots, normally feed for much of the day, while animal-feeders, such as tufted ducks, feed at certain times only.

Diving features

Most diving birds are stream-

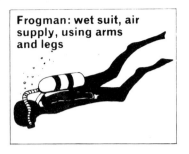

Frogman: wet suit, air supply, using arms and legs

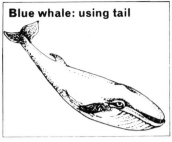

Blue whale: using tail

Tufted duck: wings held close to body, using feet

Penguin: using wings (flippers) as paddles

▲ Compare the different ways that some animals have adapted to diving and swimming underwater.

lined, with long, narrow bodies that offer little *resistance* to the water when they dive. Compare the feet, legs, feathers, wings and general shape of a diving bird with those of a land bird, such as a pheasant.

A long-tailed duck can dive to about 60 metres, and usually stays underwater for about three minutes, although it can manage about a quarter of an hour.

Protecting birds
Finally, please remember that birds are wild creatures and are very wary of being too near to people. Nesting birds will leave their eggs and young if people come too close to them for too long, and feeding birds should never be disturbed in winter, or they may starve. If you are disturbing a bird you should move away as quickly and quietly as you can.

Glossary

Adaptation The way in which creatures have evolved in order to lead their particular ways of life.

Aggression Attacking or driving away creatures from self, food, territory or mate.

Albumen The 'white' of an egg.

Bill The beak of a bird.

Binocular vision Seeing things through both eyes at once.

Bird of passage A migrating bird.

Bird of prey One which hunts other animals for food.

Breeding pair A male and a female bird who mate and produce fertile eggs.

Breeding season The time of year when birds nest and raise their young.

Brood A group of young birds hatched from one nest.

Camouflage A disguise which makes use of patterns and colours.

Census A population count.

Colony A place where many birds nest together.

Cover Concealment or a shelter for a bird or its nest.

Displaying The way birds signal to other birds and to their enemies.

Ecology The relationships of living things to each other and their surroundings.

Evolution The origination of species from other forms.

Field characters The characteristic plumage and behaviour details of a species of bird.

Field guide A book which lists detailed drawings and descriptions of different species of birds.

Flight lines The paths used by flying birds, especially on migration or to and from roosts.

Flock A group of birds, usually flying, feeding or roosting together.

Food chain The way in which a group of plants and animals are connected together because each one is a form of food for another in the group.

Food web A number of food chains, linked together at various stages.

Game birds Birds hunted by people for sport or food (like pheasants).

Gizzard Part of a bird's stomach. It often contains small stones that the bird swallows to help it digest its food.

Habitat The type of place where a particular species of animal lives, such as a seashore, oakwood or pond.

Hide A building, tent, or shelter from which people can watch birds without disturbing them.

Histogram A kind of bar chart which can show how often something happens over specified periods of time.

Incubation Keeping a fertile egg at the right temperature so that it will hatch. Birds usually do this by sitting on their eggs.

Least individual distance The distance within which a creature will not tolerate another of the same species.

Metabolism The chemical processes that take place in the body.

Migration Regular journeys of birds, usually between their breeding grounds and the places where they spend the winter.

Monocular vision Seeing things with one eye only.

Nestling A young bird that has not yet left its nest.

Ornithologist A person who studies birds.

Pellet A mass of undigested food that is regurgitated (coughed up) by a bird.

Plumage A bird's feathers.

Predator A creature that kills others for food.

Preen gland A gland situated at the base of a bird's tail, which produces an oil used by the bird when preening.

Preening The way in which a bird cleans and cares for its feathers.

Ringing Placing a small, numbered ring on the leg of a bird so that its lifespan and movements, population and breeding rate can be recorded and studied.

Roosting Periods when birds sleep or rest.

Song post A perch or other place where a bird can be heard singing.

Species A group of very similar living things that can freely interbreed in the wild. A particular species does not normally interbreed with a different species.

Summer visitors Migratory birds that visit an area for the summer only.

Territory An area defended by an individual or pair of birds against others of their species.

Thermal A current of hot, rising air.

Wader A member of the family of shorebirds.

Wildfowl Ducks, geese and swans.

Winter visitors Migratory birds that visit a country for the winter only.

Index

Page numbers in *italics* refer to illustrations.